THE
LEGISLATIVE
VETO

THE
LEGISLATIVE
VETO
Unseparating the powers

John R. Bolton

American Enterprise Institute for Public Policy Research
Washington, D. C.

John R. Bolton is engaged in the private practice of law in Washington, D. C.

ISBN 0-8447-3245-1

Library of Congress Catalog Card No. 77-75957

AEI studies 148

Printed in the United States of America

CONTENTS

INTRODUCTION

As the federal government has grown in size and power, the effects of such growth on the structure of the national government have provoked considerable interest. There is concern not only about the dangers of overconcentration of power in the hands of the central government but also about the misallocation of that power among the three branches. These concerns have spawned efforts to develop a method for preventing the use of such powers in an essentially unchecked fashion. One device that is now, perhaps, more popular than ever is the "legislative veto." [1]

The legislative veto is typically applied to the proposed regulations of independent or executive agencies. In some cases, however, the veto has been made applicable to particular agency actions, for example, decisions of the attorney general to suspend deportation proceedings against individual aliens.[2] In other cases, the legislative veto has been purportedly used to terminate authority previously granted to the executive branch.[3] The forms the legislative veto has taken vary widely, depending on the answers to two basic questions: first, by what body is the veto exercised; and second, how must that body act, that is, must it approve the proposed executive action, or disapprove it?

Considering those cases in which the full houses of Congress are involved, there are four possibilities for structuring the veto: first, the proposed executive action can be precluded if *either* house passes

---

[1] See, for example, Mary Russell, "Hill Increasingly Taking Veto Weapon into Its Own Hands," *Washington Post*, September 5, 1976, p. A10. According to this survey, legislative vetoes were enacted on the average of three times a year between 1932 and 1968. Since 1968, there have been 99 new statutes with congressional veto provisions, for a total of at least 295 such statutes.

[2] 8 U.S.C., section 1254(c)(2).

[3] See, for example, The Lend-Lease Act of 1941, 55 Stat. 32 (1941).

a resolution explicitly *disapproving* it; [4] second, the proposed executive action can be precluded if *both* houses pass resolutions of *disapproval*; [5] third, if *either* house *approves* the proposal, it is permitted to go into effect; [6] and fourth, if both houses *approve* the proposed action, it is permitted.[7]

In addition to lodging the veto power in one or both houses, numerous statutes confer it on a committee of one or both houses.[8] Although the committee veto obviously raises serious questions that merit extensive consideration, it will not be treated separately here. Virtually everything that can be said which raises questions about the legislative veto by means of a one- or two-house resolution applies all the more to the committee veto.[9] While he was still head of the Office of Legal Counsel, Justice William H. Rehnquist commented on the committee veto by saying, "I subscribe unreservedly to the notion that this particular type of provision is a violation of the constitutional principle of separation of powers." [10] The key constitutional issue is the validity of the one- or two-house legislative veto.

Likewise, statutory provisions that purportedly give Congress the power to veto less than all of a proposed regulation or action will not be separately treated.[11] The "line-item" legislative veto is, on its

---

4 See, for example, 2 U.S.C., section 483(c), and 26 U.S.C., sections 9009(c), 9039(c), providing for congressional review of proposed regulations by the Federal Election Commission (FEC).

5 The Trade Expansion Act of 1962, P.L. No. 87-794, section 351, 76 Stat. 899 (1962); 19 U.S.C., section 1981. If the President fails to proclaim an increased tariff duty or other import restriction after an affirmative finding of the Tariff Commission, he must submit to Congress a report explaining his action. Congress disapproves the President's rejection of the Tariff Commission's finding by passing, within sixty legislative days of the submission of the President's report, a concurrent resolution endorsing the Tariff Commission's position.

6 This alternative does not appear to have been employed to date.

7 See, for example, 23 U.S.C., section 104(b)(5) (approval of funds for the federal interstate highway system).

8 See, for example, Post Office Department Appropriation Act, 1971, P.L. No. 91-422, 84 Stat. 876. Appropriations to design and build new postal facilities are available only at locations approved by the Committees on Public Works of the House of Representatives and of the Senate.

9 See Joseph Harris, *Congressional Control of Administration* (Washington: Brookings Institution, 1964), pp. 213-38.

10 Remarks of William H. Rehnquist, "Committee Veto: Fifty Years of Sparring between the Executive and the Legislature," before the American Bar Association's Section of Administrative Law (Dallas, Texas, August 12, 1969), p. 5.

11 See, for example, 2 U.S.C., section 359 (which apparently permits one house of Congress to allow some proposed pay increases while prohibiting others). A provision that would have allowed a part of proposed Federal Election Commission regulations to be vetoed was proposed, H.R. 12406, 94th Congress, 2d session, section 110(b)(1) (1976), but it was not adopted.

face, indistinguishable from the normal legislative consideration of amendments to a bill under consideration. Most legislative vetoes do not contain such line-item veto provisions, and the commentators have not analyzed them in any great detail. Nonetheless, these too represent cases of *a fortiori* unconstitutionality. If preventing all of a proposed executive initiative to go forward interferes with prerogatives of the executive, then selective disapproval (which, if adroitly done, can completely alter the impact of a proposed regulation) is simply that much greater, and less justifiable, an interference.

Although the numerous forms taken by the legislative veto are quite varied, and although its scope has been a matter of considerable experimentation, its conceptual foundations have remained relatively constant. So, too, have the objections to the legislative veto remained fixed, despite its many changes in form. The basic objections are that the congressional actions intimately affect the administration of previously passed statutes, and that they are not subject, under the legislative-veto statutes, to the veto power of the President.

This study examines the practical justifications advanced on behalf of the legislative veto and the constitutional implications of its widespread use. Generally, it concludes that the veto does not achieve the pragmatic objectives set for it, and indeed may well promote precisely the opposite effects. Constitutionally, the veto is found wanting because of its distortion of the distribution of authority within the federal government and its violation of the separation of powers. Suggestions for appropriate alternatives to the veto are presented, suggestions not only consistent with the Constitution but, it is hoped, more efficacious in protecting the twin values supposedly served by the veto—a limited and responsible government whose powers are allocated in accordance with the constitutional plan.

1

THE LEGISLATIVE VETO AS A RESPONSE TO THE GROWTH OF GOVERNMENT

Until the arrival of the New Deal, the growth of government was constitutionally checked by several considerations. One was the doctrine of substantive due process, which was employed typically when economic regulations were considered. Substantive due process permitted federal courts to examine not only whether the statutes were procedurally fair but also whether the legislation had a real and substantial relation to the goals set for it. Substantive due process was often used to invalidate state and federal statutes.[1] Another important bulwark was the commerce clause (Article I, Section 8), which gives Congress the power "[t]o regulate Commerce with foreign Nations, and among the several States." The commerce clause was often interpreted to prevent the federal government from legislating in areas thought to be reserved to the states or in which no governmental intervention was warranted.[2] In addition, the general concept of federalism, supported by the Tenth Amendment, was used to restrain activity of the federal government.[3]

The "delegation of powers" doctrine was often used in conjunction with these theories. According to this doctrine, legislative

---

[1] See, for example, Lochner v. New York, 198 U.S. 45 (1905) (declaring unconstitutional a New York statute prohibiting bakery employees from working more than sixty hours a week); Adair v. United States, 208 U.S. 161 (1908) (declaring unconstitutional a federal prohibition of "yellow dog" contracts on interstate railroads).

[2] See Hammer v. Dagenhart, 247 U.S. 251 (1918) (striking down a federal statute barring the use of child labor to produce goods shipped in interstate commerce); Railroad Retirement Bd. v. Alton R. Co., 295 U.S. 30 (1935) (holding that a federal statute requiring all carriers subject to the Interstate Commerce Act to establish retirement and pension plans was unconstitutional).

[3] United States v. Butler, 297 U.S. 1 (1936) (striking down the Agricultural Adjustment Act of 1933).

authority could not be "delegated" to the executive branch to implement: "That Congress cannot delegate legislative power to the President is a principle universally recognized as vital to the integrity and maintenance of the system of government ordained by the Constitution." [4] This doctrine is directed not so much to limiting the totality of power that might be vested in the national government as it is to maintaining the proper allocation among the branches of whatever powers were held to be legitimately bestowed.

Nevertheless, the constraint imposed by barring improper delegations was punctured by several holes (as were the theories of substantive due process, restrictions on congressional power under the commerce clause, and restraints on the growth of the central government based on the concept of federalism). Congress could delegate to the President, for instance, if the executive's only functions were to act on a specific contingency,[5] or if the executive were to "fill up the details" of a general congressional scheme,[6] or in accordance with several other "exceptions" to the doctrine. As time passed, these doctrines eroded more precipitously. Substantive due process in the area of economic regulation was all but formally interred during the New Deal by several Supreme Court decisions.[7] Similiarly, power to legislate under the commerce clause received sweeping judicial approval.[8] Although considerations of federalism still retain considerable vitality, they have not been deemed sufficient to invalidate regulations implicating something that is at least arguably in the national interest.[9]

Although the national government's constitutional ability to assume major new responsibilities was thus considerably augmented,

---

[4] Field v. Clark, 143 U.S. 649, 692 (1892). (The Tariff Act of 1890 provided that the President could invoke a "retaliatory" tariff schedule against any nation that treated American products unfairly, and that the retaliatory duties were to remain in effect until the President decided to rescind them. The Supreme Court upheld this provision.)

[5] Ibid.

[6] See, for example, United States v. Grimaud, 220 U.S. 506 (1911) (sustaining a delegation to the secretary of agriculture to make regulations and take necessary steps to protect public lands from fires and other disasters).

[7] See, for example, Nebbia v. New York, 291 U.S. 502 (1934) (upholding a New York statute establishing a commission to fix maximum and minimum prices for the retail sale of milk products); West Coast Hotel Co. v. Parrish, 300 U.S. 379 (1937) (upholding a State of Washington minimum wage law).

[8] See, for example, NLRB v. Jones & Laughlin Steel Corp., 301 U.S. 1 (1937) (upholding the National Labor Relations Act of 1935); Wickard v. Filburn, 317 U.S. 11 (1942) (sustaining the Agricultural Adjustment Act of 1938).

[9] See, for example, Steward Machine Co. v. Davis, 301 U.S. 548 (1937) (sustaining the Social Security Act); Helvering v. Davis, 301 U.S. 619 (1937) (also upholding the Social Security Act).

the issue of allocating that power within the government was not necessarily thereby determined. Nonetheless, a similar pattern did emerge, involving the breakdown of the separation-of-powers doctrine. This breakdown began just prior to the New Deal in *J. W. Hampton, Jr. & Co. v. United States.*[10] Under the Tariff Act of 1922, the President had broad discretion to alter existing tariff rates if so doing would equalize the costs of American and foreign commodities. While ostensibly adhering to the delegation-of-powers doctrine, the Supreme Court ultimately upheld the Tariff Act of 1922 by saying "[i]f Congress shall lay down by legislative act an intelligible principle to which the person or body authorized to . . . [proceed] is directed to conform, such legislative action is not a forbidden delegation of legislative power."[11]

Confronted with a wide variety of new programs during the New Deal, the Supreme Court did find excessive, unconstitutional delegations of power in two cases.[12] In one of those cases, Justice Benjamin N. Cardozo complained:

> The delegated power of the legislation which has found expression in this code is not canalized within banks that keep it from overflowing. It is unconfined and vagrant . . . not confined to any single act nor to any class or group of acts identified or described by reference to a standard. Here in effect is a roving commission to inquire into evils and upon discovery correct them.[13]

Despite these two decisions, and despite even stronger opposition to improper delegation in the states, the Supreme Court has not found any other delegations of power to the executive unconstitutional.[14] In fact, the doctrine has fallen into such disrepute that a respected administrative-law commentator has warned attorneys not to raise it on behalf of their clients.[15]

---

[10] 276 U.S. 394 (1928).

[11] Ibid., p. 409.

[12] Panama Refining Co. v. Ryan, 293 U.S. 388 (1935) (holding unconstitutional a section of the National Industrial Recovery Act of 1933); Schechter Poultry Corp. v. United States, 295 U.S. 495 (1935) (declaring unconstitutional another section of that same statute).

[13] Schechter Poultry Corp. v. United States, p. 551 (Cardozo, J., concurring).

[14] See generally, Walter Gellhorn and Clark Byse, *Administrative Law; Cases and Comments*, 5th edition (Mineola, New York: The Foundation Press, 1970), pp. 48-82.

[15] "Lawyers who try to win cases by arguing that congressional delegations are unconstitutional almost invariably do more harm than good to their clients' interests. . . . The vaguest of standards are held adequate, and various delegations

This brief survey of the growth of judicial acceptance of wide-ranging administrative powers emphasizes a crucial point: the delegation of immense authority, authority not restrained by narrow and precise standards, could not have been achieved without the acquiescence of the legislative branch. More ambitious attempts of the executive to act without congressional support have been uniformly and emphatically rejected by the Supreme Court, as in the cases concerning President Harry S Truman's seizure of the nation's steel mills and President Richard M. Nixon's secret White House tape recordings.[16]

Yet now, ironically, sentiment in favor of widespread use of the legislative veto is most strongly concentrated in the Congress, and its most articulate spokesmen stress that one of their primary intentions in supporting the veto is precisely to restrain overly exuberant administrative agencies. As Representative Elliott H. Levitas (Democrat, Georgia), sponsor of comprehensive legislation to apply the legislative veto to administrative regulations that trigger statutorily imposed criminal provisions, said during the congressional hearings:

> The federal bureaucracy has evolved into a fourth—non-Constitutional—branch of government, with a thick tangle of regulations that carry the force of law without benefit of legislative consideration.
>
> I frankly do not believe that the precepts of a free society are compatible with the situation whereby Congress continues to permit civil servants or appointed officials to conjure up thousands upon thousands of far-reaching laws that can put citizens in jeopardy of liberty or property without having anyone elected by the people involved in the process.[17]

Representative Levitas's statement is one of a long line of congressional complaints about the actions of administrative agencies that propose as their solution the implementation of the legislative veto,

---

without standards have been upheld." K. C. Davis, *Administrative Law Treatise* sec. 2.01 (Saint Paul, Minnesota: West Publishing Co., 1958). But see National Cable Television Assn. v. United States, 415 U.S. 336 (1974).

[16] *Youngstown Sheet & Tube Co. v. Sawyer*, 343 U.S. 579 (1952); *United States v. Nixon*, 418 U.S. 683 (1974).

[17] Statement of Representative Elliott H. Levitas, *Hearings before the Subcommittee on Administrative Law and Government Relations of the House Committee on the Judiciary on H.R. 3658, H.R. 8231, and Related Bills*, 94th Congress, 1st session, section 141 (1975) (hereinafter referred to as *Congressional Review of Administrative Rulemaking*). Representative Levitas was the sponsor of H.R. 3658.

even though it was legislative action that gave the executive agencies the ability to act in the fashion now complained about.

During the period of the late New Deal, the legislative veto made its first important appearances in domestic affairs. Interestingly, it was included in the Reorganization Act of 1939, a statute providing for methods to effect major alterations in the structure of the executive branch.[18] The first important use of the legislative veto in the field of foreign relations came during consideration of U.S. entry into the League of Nations. It was suggested that the treaty embodying U.S. membership in the League allow for possible U.S. withdrawal at some future point by means of a concurrent resolution. Since the treaty was not adopted, the suggestion was never implemented.[19]

Thus, Congress turned to the legislative veto at crucial points in the international and domestic history of the nation, at points when the executive branch assumed (or attempted to assume) new and greater responsibilities than it had previously undertaken. Following the Reorganization Act of 1939 came what one commentator has called "an almost explosive increase in the use of concurrent resolution provisions as a means of controlling executive powers and actions."[20] In particular, the legislative veto was employed to cover programs or actions involving the disposition of government property, the making of government contracts, and the construction of federal facilities.[21]

Although the Democrats controlled both houses of Congress for the last six years of President Dwight D. Eisenhower's term, conflicts between the two branches on a constitutional level were not inordinately frequent. When President Nixon assumed office, the Democratic Party still controlled Congress, but a new set of circumstances prevailed. The legislative branch had grown accustomed to asserting its independence of the executive during the debate over the Vietnam War. The additional partisan motivation with a Republican as President was later joined by the weakening of executive power during the Watergate-caused crisis at the end of Nixon's administration and the beginning of Ford's. Into this breach flowed numerous legis-

---

[18] A detailed examination of the history of the reorganization acts is provided in Robert W. Ginnane, "The Control of Federal Administration by Congressional Resolutions and Committees," *Harvard Law Review*, vol. 66 (1953), pp. 576-82. The most comprehensive and detailed history to date of the legislative veto is H. Lee Watson, "Congress Steps Out: A Look at Congressional Control of the Executive," *California Law Review*, vol. 63 (1975), p. 983.

[19] Ginnane, "Control of Federal Administration," note 18, p. 575.

[20] Watson, "Congress Steps Out," p. 1014. Watson also details the growth of "committee-veto" procedures whereby one committee of the Senate or House in effect wields the veto power for the larger bodies. Ibid., pp. 1017-29.

[21] These provisions generally involved committee vetoes. Ibid., pp. 1018-25.

lative vetoes.[22] In consequence, by 1976 extensive hearings had been held on proposals that would extend the legislative veto to virtually all administrative agencies, and the House nearly passed such legislation that year.[23]

The reaction of American Presidents to these developments has been, not surprisingly, essentially political. When necessary or convenient, they have acquiesced in the use of a legislative veto; when possible, they have vetoed legislation containing it, often with ringing declarations of principled regard for the separation of powers.[24] Perhaps the most interesting analysis of the essentially political nature of the executive decisions was provided by Supreme Court Justice Robert H. Jackson.[25] When Jackson was President Franklin D. Roosevelt's attorney general, Roosevelt had been faced with a difficult

---

22 Ibid., pp. 1016-17, note 160, and p. 1029.

23 See generally *Congressional Review of Administrative Rulemaking.* See also *Hearings before the Senate Committee on Government Operations on S. 2258 et al.,* 94th Congress, 2d session (1976) (hereinafter referred to as *Improving Congressional Oversight*). The bill that nearly passed the House on September 21, 1976 (H.R. 12048) was a composite introduced by Representative Walter Flowers (Democrat, Alabama). Because the proposal had become tied up in the House Rules Committee, its supporters were required to follow a procedure mandating a two-thirds vote of approval from the full House for the bill to pass. Richard E. Cohen, "Watchdog or Wastrel," *National Journal*, October 2, 1976, p. 1398. The final vote was 265-135, or just short of the required majority. *Congressional Record*, vol. 122 (daily ed., September 21, 1976), pp. H 10718-19.

24 For instance, President Gerald R. Ford signed the Presidential Recordings and Materials Preservation Act, P.L. 93-526, 88 Stat. 1695 (1974), which included a veto provision, section 104(b)(1), without even mentioning the existence of that provision in his description of the bill. See *Weekly Compilation of Presidential Documents*, vol. 10 (December 23, 1974), p. 1595. President Ford was, at that time, under intense criticism for having pardoned former President Nixon. In May of 1976, however, President Ford vetoed S. 2662, the Foreign Assistance Bill of 1976, in large measure because it "would seriously obstruct the exercise of the President's constitutional responsibilities for the conduct of foreign affairs." *Weekly Compilation of Presidential Documents*, vol. 12 (May 10, 1976), p. 828. Other proposals vetoed by President Ford because of the inclusion of legislative-veto provisions in proposed statutes include: H.R. 12944, a measure extending funding under the Federal Insecticide, Fungicide and Rodenticide Act for six months, *Weekly Compilation of Presidential Documents*, vol. 12 (August 13, 1976), p. 1261; H.R. 12567, a bill appropriating funds under the Federal Fire Prevention and Control Act of 1974 for two years, ibid. (July 7, 1976) p. 1142; and H.R. 5446, a proposal providing for implementation of U.S. obligations under the Convention on the International Regulations for Preventing Collisions at Sea, ibid. (October 10, 1976), p. 1486. The constitutionality of the Presidential Recordings and Materials Preservation Act was challenged by former President Nixon in *Nixon v. Administrator of General Services*, 408 F. Supp. 321 (D.D.C. 1976) probable jurisdiction noted, 45 U.S.L.W. 3399 (November 29, 1976). In the view of the three-judge court, it was not necessary to decide the constitutionality of the legislative-veto provision. 408 F. Supp. 321, 338, note 17.

25 Robert H. Jackson, "A Presidential Legal Opinion," *Harvard Law Review*, vol. 66 (1953), p. 1353.

decision because of a legislative-veto provision in the Lend-Lease Act. Justice Jackson labeled the provision "constitutionally objectionable but politically necessary."

Obviously, Lend-Lease was something President Roosevelt ardently desired, but the inclusion of a provision allowing Congress to terminate the program by means of a concurrent resolution caused him to fear "the long-range effect of the precedent on the balance of power between Congress and the Executive." Roosevelt asked Jackson to prepare a memorandum for his signature on the unconstitutionality of the provision as some way to undercut any precedent-setting value its inclusion in the Lend-Lease Act might have. The memorandum stressed a point central to the constitutional debate over the congressional veto:

> In effect, this provision is an attempt by Congress to authorize a repeal by means of a concurrent resolution of the two Houses, of certain provisions of an Act of Congress. . . . The Constitution contains no provision whereby the Congress may legislate by concurrent resolution without the approval of the President.[26]

Roosevelt was objecting to the congressional attempt to legislate while also avoiding the possibility of a presidential veto. Rather than following the normal pattern, Congress was trying to bypass the veto power and thus eliminate the President's role in the legislative process. Jackson did not reveal the memorandum until after Roosevelt's death because he had been charged to keep it secret until a time "when it would not embarrass his followers or give comfort to his adversaries." [27]

Even though a secret presidential memorandum is a highly unusual and unorthodox way to resist unconstitutional incursions on the prerogatives of the executive, even more unorthodox tactics were to follow. Confronted with a "committee veto" provision in the Small Reclamation Projects Act of 1956, President Eisenhower announced that, although he intended to sign the legislation, he expected Congress to remove the offending provision as soon as it reconvened. Moreover, although the secretary of the interior would begin his review of suggested project proposals, he would take no action until the veto was removed or revised. President Eisenhower suggested that, if Congress wished to review the programs, it require the Interior

---

[26] Ibid., p. 1358.
[27] Ibid., p. 1357.

Department "to submit such reports as it may find of value in carrying on its legislative functions." [28] Similarly, President Lyndon B. Johnson directed his secretary of agriculture not to make any loans pursuant to certain 1966 amendments to the Bankhead-Jones Farm Tenant Act. Those amendments provided that no loans under the act could be made unless the House Committee on Agriculture and the Senate Committee on Agriculture and Forestry both approved such loans by resolution.[29]

President Gerald R. Ford provided an even more interesting case. The 1974 amendments to the Federal Election Campaign Act contained a legislative veto. When President Ford signed these amendments, he questioned whether some sections of the legislation might not be in violation of the First Amendment, but he made no comments regarding the legislative veto.[30] When the 1976 amendments were passed, they in effect reenacted the legislative-veto provisions. President Ford signed the 1976 amendments as well, but once again he expressed constitutional reservations, this time about the legislative veto. In addition to simply expressing his doubts, he "directed the Attorney General to challenge the constitutionality of this provision at the earliest possible opportunity." [31]

Although it would have been more straightforward for Presidents Roosevelt, Eisenhower, Johnson, and Ford to veto the offending legislation, their views of practical politics and the importance of the legislation under consideration rendered such action impossible. The exigencies of the situations effectively required presidential approval despite the distasteful presence of the veto, and the judiciary should recognize this when it is called upon to judge the congressional veto's validity. The President hardly gives his constitutional blessing to a provision he is forced to accept as part of an essentially political accommodation. Although the Framers of the Constitution justifiably expected that the two elected branches would solve most separation-of-powers questions politically, they did not intend that the judicial branch should stand by while one of the elected branches acted beyond its constitutional limits. Nor does the fact that the legislative

[28] Dwight D. Eisenhower, *Public Papers of the President of the United States, 1956*, section 165 (Washington: Federal Register Division, National Archives and Records Services, General Services Administration, 1958), p. 650.

[29] *Weekly Compilation of Presidential Documents*, vol. 2 (November 8, 1966), pp. 1676-77.

[30] *Weekly Compilation of Presidential Documents*, vol. 11 (October 21, 1974), p. 1285.

[31] *Weekly Compilation of Presidential Documents*, vol. 12 (May 11, 1976), p. 858.

veto has been frequently employed make it valid: "That an unconstitutional action has been taken before surely does not render that same action any less unconstitutional at a later date." [32]

---

[32] Powell v. McCormack, 395 U.S. 486, 546-74 (1969). Given the relatively recent emergence of the legislative veto, the Supreme Court's further comment in *Powell* regarding certain earlier exclusion cases that "the precedential value of these cases tends to increase in proportion to their proximity to the Convention in 1787," 395 U.S., p. 547, is certainly also pertinent. See statement of Assistant Attorney General Antonin Scalia in *Improving Congressional Oversight*, p. 126.

2

THE RATIONALE FOR
THE LEGISLATIVE VETO

Unlike so many issues involving governmental regulations of various aspects of our affairs, there is no serious dispute between proponents and opponents of the legislative veto on one key point: the administrative agencies have such an awesome range of powers, and they act with such disturbing frequency in contravention of legislative intent, that some additional controls must be imposed upon them. The real issue, therefore, is not the goal to be attained but rather the method or methods best suited to attain the goal. This section treats some of the justifications offered for the congressional veto, both from a pragmatic viewpoint and as a backdrop against which constitutional considerations can be measured later.

Preserving the Legislative Intent

A uniform complaint of supporters of the legislative veto is that the agencies charged with enforcing or implementing legislation often ignore the legislative intent underlying the legislation. The following examples are taken from the 1976 congressional hearings on *Administrative Rulemaking:*

> The Department of Labor is required by the Davis-Bacon Act of 1931 to set minimum wage rates for federally funded or federally assisted projects at the level prevailing in the area of the project. A study done by the General Accounting Office in 1970 indicated that Congress had intended the Labor Department to set the rates in accordance with local rates for residential construction. However, in fixing minimum wage rates for the construction of federally financed housing projects, the Department had adopted the prevailing

local rates for commercial construction, which were significantly higher than the rates for residential construction. The erroneous determination by the Department resulted in extra costs of at least $1.4 million in the District of Columbia during 1965 to 1967, and in extra costs of over $2 million in seven housing projects in four states.[1]

The Army Corps of Engineers had been authorized to promulgate regulations to implement certain sections of the Federal Water Pollution Control Act (regulating soil dumping into navigable waterways). As one member put it,

> "[w]hat was intended by Congress to be a relatively simple permit system was to become an all-encompassing land use management program under the corps' regulations. Here was a situation in which Congress had not even passed land use planning legislation—and yet the bureaucracy by regulation was instituting massive land use management and control." [2]

The National Park Service of the Department of the Interior proposed regulations that would ban motorless aircraft from flying over national parks. From one member's perspective,

> "[t]here is no requirement in the law that an aircraft have a motor to fly in the national parks. The intent of Congress and the law is clear. The Park Service is attempting to justify the regulation by publishing three indistinct reasons which have little bearing on the need for regulation and fail to justify the noncompliance with the law." [3]

These examples form only a small percentage of the total number of bureaucratic "outrages" presented. In by far the greatest number of cases, the problem was not that an agency had acted contrary to explicit legislative intent, but that the agency had simply acted in a fashion that disturbed a particular member of Congress (or, more likely, one of his constituents who had brought the matter to his attention).

Witnesses complained, for instance, of Environmental Protection Agency regulations that stringently restricted parking in downtown Boston during peak commuting hours; of the Equal Employment

---

[1] Statement of Representative John B. Breckenridge (Democrat, Kentucky), *Congressional Review of Administrative Rulemaking*, p. 206 (citing two Government Accounting Office reports).

[2] Testimony of Representative Gillis W. Long (Democrat, Louisiana), ibid., p. 186.

[3] Statement of Representative G. William Whitehurst (Republican, Virginia), ibid., p. 191.

Opportunity Commission's requiring the Houston police force to hire without regard to prior criminal convictions; [4] of decisions by the Consumer Product Safety Commission mandating stricter standards for the construction of "walk-behind" power lawn mowers that would significantly increase their costs; [5] of overly exacting child/staff ratios required by regulations of the Department of Health, Education and Welfare; [6] and of numerous regulations of the Occupational Safety and Health Administration. [7]

Whether or not any of these complaints has substantive merit, it is plain that they emphasize the deep congressional dissatisfaction with agency performance and with the extent to which the lives of individual citizens are now affected by the federal government. As Representative Walter Flowers (Democrat, Alabama) put it:

> The multitude of rules and regulations issued by Federal departments and agencies have an increasing impact and effect upon our citizens. Repeatedly at the hearings on this legislation, witnesses testified as to the extent Federal regulations affect average citizens and impose a considerable degree of governmental interference in their lives. [8]

In many respects, regulations that possibly violate the legislative intent and regulations that are irritating, burdensome, seemingly capricious, or hard to understand meld together in the congressional mind. And, after all, the assertion that an agency is really not acting the way it was "supposed to" is a convenient excuse to avoid responsibility for an agency that is then annoying one's constituents.

Even if it is agreed, however, that the administrative agencies need to be restrained, the question still remains what it is about the legislative veto that will accomplish that goal, or why it is that other means would not be more efficacious. Would it not be more sensible at the outset to define more carefully the role and authority of agencies charged with implementing new programs, in effect making the legislative intent more explicit in the statutory authority? And, if faced with a situation in which an agency acted in a way that a majority of the Congress felt was contrary to its intent, would not

---

[4] Statement of Representative Levitas, ibid., pp. 141-42.

[5] Statement of Representative Willis D. Gradison, Jr. (Republican, Ohio), ibid., p. 193.

[6] Statement of Representative W. Henson Moore (Republican, Louisiana), ibid., p. 232.

[7] See, for example, statement of Representative Jack T. Brinkley (Democrat, Georgia), ibid., p. 174.

[8] *Congressional Record*, vol. 122 (daily ed., September 21, 1976), p. H 10668.

amendatory legislation clarifying that intent (without necessarily having to prescribe every last detail of the regulatory scheme) be an appropriate remedy?

Although the answers to these questions ought to be affirmative, they would be bitter medicine for Congress to take. The first reason for this is that Congress often finds it politically useful to slough off a problem by creating an administrative agency to undertake some deliberately vague mandate at some undetermined point in the future. It is far easier to decide to have someone else decide than it is to make difficult choices on specific issues. As just noted, members of Congress may be unable to distinguish between regulations that violate the legislative intent and regulations that are simply wrong-headed. This phenomenon is not accidental. Legislators may well not fully understand what they are voting on when they pass statutes in the first place. It should cause little wonder that they cannot remember several years later what they intended to do at the time of passage.

The second reason is that legislation requires participation by the President, and he may well not be inclined to agree with substantial alterations in the statutes affected. It is far more convenient simply to energize one (or, if need be, both) of the houses to oppose a particular regulation.

A third possible reason is that Congress lacks the expertise to engage in the kind of lawmaking suggested, that it must rely on the agencies to develop the bulk of the detailed regulations. There is certainly substance to this contention, but it is somewhat beside the point. Congress is surely expert enough to formulate statutory general policy that would prevent undesirable regulations from appearing again. The Internal Revenue Code of 1954 is a plain example of both how detailed Congress can be and how great an expertise it can acquire if it chooses to do so. More specifically, Congress can act with surgical precision when it cares to, as when it reversed *by statute* a regulation of the National Highway Traffic and Safety Administration requiring seatbelt interlocks.[9]

The objections to a more exacting role for Congress in the drafting and amending of statutes are thus essentially arguments of convenience: the legislative veto is easier, easier politically and easier mentally. However much one may sympathize with the arduousness of a politician's life, that sympathy does not justify permitting the Congress to abstain from its responsibilities at the time of drafting statutes in the hope that an alert staff member will espy administrative avoidance of legislative intent several years later.

---

[9] Motor Vehicle and Schoolbus Safety Amendment of 1974, 88 Stat. 1470.

Protecting Citizens from Unaccountable Power

Another theme in the congressional consideration of legislative vetoes is the notion that the bureaucracy, because it is not elected, is not politically "accountable" to the people. The agencies never have to defend themselves against opponents for election, they need not appear in public to debate their proposed regulations, and they often behave in decidedly "independent" ways. Representative M. Caldwell Butler (Republican, Virginia) summarized much of the commentary on the accountability issue when he said:

> we have delegated the power to enforce these laws, often with little in the way of guidance, to the unelected bureaucracy. . . . We are still faced with a situation where the government, largely through the actions of unelected and unaccountable persons, is directing the use of a considerable part of our economic resources.[10]

In many respects, these complaints are part of the general distaste for the growth of governmental power—or dislike for the "imperial presidency."[11] Such concerns are of considerable importance, and there is now widespread agreement with the idea that the accretion of federal power ought not to continue unabated, and that exercises of existing power ought to be made more accountable. The legislative veto is thus offered as a way to make the bureaucracy responsible for its actions.

At least some of these demands for political accountability should be taken skeptically. Representative Jack F. Kemp (Republican, New York) quite candidly pointed out that the average citizen cannot vent his frustrations against the agencies themselves, but only by "voting against those few upon which they can have an influence through the ballot box—a Congressman, a Senator, a Presidential candidate—no matter how much those few might have disagreed with and actually fought the decisions of the bureaucracy giving rise to those frustrations."[12] There is thus at least a certain amount of self-interest

---

[10] Testimony of Representative M. Caldwell Butler, *Congressional Review of Administrative Rulemaking*, pp. 178-79. See also statement of Representative James R. Mann (Democrat, South Carolina), ibid., p. 190; statement of Representative G. William Whitehurst (Republican, Virginia), ibid., p. 192; statement of Representative Robert W. Kasten, Jr. (Republican, Wisconsin), ibid., p. 194; statement of Representative Charles Thone (Republican, Nebraska), ibid., p. 221; statement of Representative Jack F. Kemp (Republican, New York), ibid., p. 221.

[11] See, for example, Arthur M. Schlesinger, Jr., *The Imperial Presidency* (Boston: Houghton Mifflin Co., Inc., 1973).

[12] Statement of Representative Kemp, *Congressional Review of Administrative Rulemaking*, p. 221.

involved in congressional concern over the lack of accountability of the agencies.

Such self-interest, however, is certainly not to be discouraged. Its underlying concern is well founded and important. The suggestion has often been made that, if Congress were ever to subject itself to the statutes it imposes on the rest of the populace, its views on the desirability of ever greater federal regulation would be considerably altered. The electoral uneasiness that senators and representatives feel when they see the work of their handcrafted agencies can only contribute toward a more realistic view on the limits of governmental effectiveness. Nonetheless, resorting to the legislative veto as a palliative is hardly an adequate response.

Surely, if Congress fails to veto (or explicitly accepts) regulations that develop later into opprobrious restraints, its members will be just as much subject to castigation as if they had never played any role at all. Moreover, the inclusion of provisions in proposed legislation asserting that failure to veto creates no presumption of congressional approval will be of little popular effect. However the courts may construe such a provision, the citizens are as unlikely to accept such an exculpatory clause as they are now to accept protestations of congressional impotence. In either case, the accountability of the agencies will not have been increased.

In addition, there is every reason to believe that providing one more opportunity to defeat proposed regulations, which presumably may be quite unpalatable to certain interests, will encourage still more abuse to the legislative process than exists now. One need not accept the theory that undesirable "special interests" dominate government life to believe that groups and businesses with considerable financial, philosophical, or social interests at stake will make every effort to exert their influence. Delay alone would make the administrative process even more unresponsive and difficult to manage than it is now. A hypothetical colloquy read to a Senate committee hearing amply demonstrates the "procedural quagmire" entailed by the legislative veto:

> [AGENCY] CHAIRMAN. What a great day! The Commission has finally reached unanimous agreement on the airline overbooking rule, and voted to issue it at once.
>
> GENERAL COUNSEL. We have been working on this for years, but it's worth it because the rule is really a good one.
>
> CHAIRMAN. The public has been very critical of us for not having dealt with this problem years ago. Also there has

been tremendous pressure on us from members of Congress, demanding that we get the rule out.

GENERAL COUNSEL. Even the industry leaders want us to get done with the matter.

CHAIRMAN. The Commission wants to get this into effect immediately. We must give a specific effective date because the airlines need sufficient lead time to program their computers. How soon can we put the rule in force?

GENERAL COUNSEL. I don't know.[13]

Although offered in a humorous vein, the imaginary dialogue sounded uncomfortably realistic.

Clearly, the administrative agencies can and should be made accountable in ways far superior to the legislative veto. For instance, the so-called independent agencies could be brought more or less explicitly under the control of the executive branch. Commentators who have advocated this approach argue:

> The premise that underlies the proposal is that some increase in the President's ability to intervene openly when he deems the issue sufficiently important will make him chargeable with political responsibility for the agency's action, and will make him accountable for not intervening when the electorate thinks he should.[14]

Although these same observers propose a one-house legislative veto—also in the name of greater accountability—one of them has stated his belief that the veto will likely be declared unconstitutional.[15] Another method of ensuring accountability is more attention by the Senate to appointments. Instead of routine confirmation proceedings, much closer care should be paid to the views and intentions of presidential nominees. A precise and detailed examination of an appointee's outlook could have a much more lasting impression on his actions than occasional and sporadic resort to the legislative veto.[16]

It also remains to be explained why other, more traditional means of oversight—the investigatory hearings, control over agency budgets, and the like—have failed. What has in fact failed are not these methods but the Congress itself, as is shown by the congressional hearings that considered the legislative veto (and particularly

---

[13] *Improving Congressional Oversight*, pp. 167-68.

[14] Lloyd N. Cutler and David R. Johnson, "Regulation and the Political Process," *Yale Law Journal*, vol. 84 (1975), p. 1417.

[15] Testimony of Lloyd N. Cutler, *Improving Congressional Oversight*, pp. 12-13.

[16] See, for example, statement of Professor Victor Kramer, ibid., p. 324.

by the statements of the members of Congress themselves).[17] Representative Levitas cogently articulated this point:

> while Congress may solve a specific problem through delegation of its legislative power, though that is debatable, we thereby create a far more serious and extensive problem than the original one we attempted to redress.[18]

Given Congress's responsibility, in substantial measure, for the existing imbalance of power among the three branches, the focus for possible improvement ought to be on Congress and the powerful weapons it now possesses. Until these weapons have been shown to be inadequate, the case for the legislative veto is indeed weak. By turning to the legislative veto as a solution, Congress risks creating a Rube Goldberg contraption less workable than the existing system, and less likely to solve the very real problems caused by both the growth of federal power generally and the growth of presidential power specifically.[19]

Perhaps even more dangerous than the immediate effects, however, is the illusion that an easily available legislative veto would create—the illusion of congressional control. The congressional veto might well be considered a panacea, and consequently less, rather than more, care would be taken in defining new grants of power to the executive and independent agencies. This possibility has obvious ramifications for the constitutional issues surrounding the veto, as will be more fully considered later. Nonetheless, it is also of considerable importance on purely pragmatic grounds. It would be a strange reform indeed that resulted in more abuses of the kind now complained of and less accountability than presently exists.

Intimidating the Administrative Agencies

The legislative veto can be an effective device. There are several ways in which its influence can be felt, directly and indirectly. When a proposed regulation is vetoed, that action will likely be debated. In that

---

[17] See, for example, colloquy between Representatives Flowers and Del M. Clawson (Republican, California), *Congressional Review of Administrative Rulemaking*, p. 365.

[18] Ibid., p. 143.

[19] James Madison suggested that, although congressional repeal of statutes might prove difficult in some cases, limiting their duration might be a desirable alternative. Jonathan Elliot, *Elliott's Debates*, vol. 5, p. 538. Similar proposals (often called "sunset" provisions) have been made recently, but their efficacy is still uncertain.

debate, numerous voices will be heard and, in effect, new legislative history will be made. That "revisionist" history will, of course, be of considerable value to agency staff members when they attempt to draft future regulations (with an eye toward avoiding a veto of the next set of regulations). In effect, Congress will be given repeated opportunities to pour new meaning into old statutory phrases. And, by design, it will be able to engage in this essentially legislative activity without fear of subsequent presidential rebuke. For if the legislative veto is constitutional, the President will not have a veto over this legislative rewriting of the statutory history.

Equally important in the minds of adherents of the legislative veto is the ability of Congress to influence the actions of agencies without explicitly vetoing their regulations. As a matter of practical administration the inhibiting effect is crucial, for otherwise Congress would have to consider far more proposed regulations than it is probably capable of handling. Representative Levitas, in fact, stressed precisely this point:

> I think once this bill becomes a law, you are going to see a lot more self-restraint on the part of bureaucracy because now they know that the judicial process is very limited, very slow and most of their work product is going to be unchallenged but now they will know that Congress will be looking over their shoulders.[20]

There was virtually unanimous congressional agreement with this statement, and indeed the congressional reasoning seems quite correct. The possibility of a legislative veto would seem to have an effect on administrative actions somewhat analogous to the threat of a presidential veto on congressional actions. In fact, the congressional veto may well be a more pronounced threat because of the committee system in Congress. Proposed regulations would be referred typically to the congressional committee already established as having jurisdiction over the promulgating agency. Since the close working relationships that the agencies build with legislative committees are quite valuable to them, the agency members would be reluctant to cause serious impairment to their long-term relationships, except in the gravest circumstances. Congressional influence over substantive agency policy

---

[20] Testimony of Representative Levitas, *Congressional Review of Administrative Rulemaking*, pp. 160-61. James Wilson's remarks at the Constitutional Convention regarding the absolute executive veto are pertinent: "Its silent operation would therefore preserve harmony and prevent mischief." *Elliott's Debates*, vol. 5, p. 152. See also, Geoffrey S. Stewart, "Constitutionality of the Legislative Veto," *Harvard Journal of Legislation*, vol. 13 (1976), pp. 593, 613.

could thus increase considerably even without the need for messy confrontations over possible legislative vetoes.

It is precisely this kind of "intimidation" of the agencies that ought most properly to be accomplished by legislation. Congressional influence under a legislative-veto system would be manifested in meetings between members of Congress and agencies, not in full public debate. If anything, accountability would be considerably diminished because the lines of influence would be much more difficult to discern.[21] In effect, the discussion has come full circle: Congress will have acquired a way to effectuate its intent (or at least the intent of those members most interested) without ever having to divulge what that intent is.

---

[21] Professor Walter Gellhorn has warned that the legislative veto may "have the effect of pressing administrative regulations and their ultimate decisions into the private arena of congressional offices." *Congressional Review of Administrative Rulemaking*, p. 257. See also testimony of Kathleen F. O'Reilly (Legislative Director of the Consumer Federation of America), *"Improving Congressional Oversight*, pp. 451-52.

3

CONSTITUTIONAL
CONSIDERATIONS

The doctrine of separation of powers, on which so much of the structure of the national government rests, relies essentially on the "political" accommodation of the various branches. In most ways, their conflicts are resolved within, and without much damage to, the framework provided by the Constitution. But, as the Supreme Court warned in *Kilbourn* v. *Thompson*, "while the experience of almost a century has in general shown a wise and commendable forbearance in each of these branches from encroachments upon the others, it is not to be denied that such attempts have been made, and it is believed not always without success." Indeed, there are "powerful and growing temptations to those to whom that exercise is intrusted, to overstep the just boundaries of their own departments, and enter upon the domain of one of the others, or to assume powers not intrusted to either of them."[1]

The Intent of the Framers

When the Framers wrote the Constitution, they did not intend that the three branches of government conform totally to a Platonic ideal of "separation." They did not intend, for instance, to bar the Congress from any role in the appointment process, and that is why the Senate was given the advice and consent power in Article II, Section 2. In like fashion, the President was not meant to be excluded totally from the formulation of statutes, and hence the creation of the veto power.[2] As the Supreme Court said in *Buckley* v. *Valeo*, "[t]he men

---

[1] 103 U.S. 168, 191-92 (1881).

[2] Buckley v. Valeo, 424 U.S. 1, 121 (1976). See also Kilbourn v. Thompson, 103 U.S. 168, 191 ("It is also essential to the successful working of this system

who met in Philadelphia in the summer of 1787 were practical states-
men, experienced in politics, who viewed the principle of separation
of powers as a vital check against tyranny."[3] These deviations from
the model that all conceptually executive power should be vested in
the President and all conceptually legislative power should be vested
in the Congress were deliberately and carefully designed to protect each
branch against incursions of the other branches. Since in many respects the history of the presidential appointment power, addressed
in *Buckley* v. *Valeo,* and the veto are similar, and since they clearly
implicate many of the same constitutional principles, their close rela-
tionship should be borne in mind when considering the legislative veto.

It is accepted almost without contention that the Framers were
quite concerned that the President might be unable to defend himself
against legislative encroachments.[4] As Alexander Hamilton put it during the ratification debates:

> The propensity of the legislative department to intrude upon
> the rights and to absorb the powers of the other departments
> has been already suggested and repeated; the insufficiency
> or a mere parchment delineation of the boundaries of each,
> has also been remarked upon; and the necessity of furnish-
> ing each with constitutional arms for its own defense, has
> been inferred and proved. From these clear and indubitable
> principles results the propriety of a negative, either absolute
> or qualified, in the executive, upon the acts of the legislative
> branches. Without the one or the other the former would be
> absolutely unable to defend himself against the depredations
> of the latter. He might gradually be stripped of his authori-
> ties by successive resolutions, or annihilated by a single vote.
> And in the one mode or the other, the legislative and execu-
> tive powers might speedily come to be blended in the same
> hands. If even no propensity had ever discovered itself in

that the persons entrusted with power in any one of these branches shall not be
permitted to encroach upon the powers confided to the others, but that each
shall by the law of its creation be limited to the exercise of the powers appropriate to its own department and no other. To these general propositions there
are in the Constitution of the United States some important exceptions. One of
these is, that the President is so far made a part of the legislative power, that
his assent is required to the enactment of all statutes and resolutions of
Congress.")

[3] 424 U.S. 1, 121.

[4] When the Constitutional Convention convened, only South Carolina's chief
executive possessed a veto. The possibility of providing a veto power was,
however, much discussed, and some believe that a proposed Massachusetts constitution was defeated because the governor did not have a veto. Charles C.
Thach, "The Creation of the Presidency, 1775-1789," Johns Hopkins University
Studies in History and Political Science, vol. 40 (1922), pp. 415, 449-68.

the legislative body to invade the rights of the executive, the rules of just reasoning and theoretic propriety would of themselves teach us, that the one ought not be left to the mercy of the other, but ought to possess a constitutional and effectual power of self defense.[5]

Ensuring the efficacy of the veto occupied much of the Constitutional Convention's attention. For instance, was the veto to be absolute or qualified; that is, was the veto to be the final act in the legislative process, or would Congress be allowed to "override" (to use the contemporary term) the President's action?[6] If the latter, was the required vote to be a two-thirds or a three-quarters majority?[7] More importantly, was the President to exercise the veto solely on his own initiative, or was he to be required to exercise it in conjunction with several members of the judiciary (the so-called council-of-revision approach)?[8] In what one scholar has called "a decision of the first importance," the veto was granted to the President acting alone.[9]

An equally vexing question was how to ensure that the veto was not evaded by the Congress. After all, as James Madison said later:

> the great security against a gradual concentration of the several powers in the same department, consists in giving to those who administer each department, the necessary constitutional means, and personal motives, to resist encroachments of the others. The provision for defence must in this, as in all other cases, be made commensurate to the danger of attack.[10]

Madison was aware that, if the veto provision were drawn too narrowly, Congress would find it easy to avoid. He feared that the ver-

---

[5] *The Federalist*, Number 73, ed. Jacob E. Cooke (Middletown, Conn.: Wesleyan University Press, 1961), pp. 494-95.

[6] Speaking on behalf of the absolute veto, Wilson urged that without it, "the legislature can at any moment sink it [the executive] into non-existence." The absolute negative was defeated by a vote of ten states against, none in favor. A related proposal, to give the executive an absolute power to suspend the enforcement of statutes also lost 10-0. *Elliott's Debates*, vol. 5, pp. 151-55.

[7] The Convention shifted back and forth between a two-thirds and a three-quarters requirement. Ultimately, of course, a two-thirds majority of both houses was required to overrule the President's veto. Ibid., pp. 536-38.

[8] Randolph first proposed that the President "and a convenient number of the national judiciary" share the veto power. Ibid., p. 128. Although a general decision to lodge the executive authority in one person was made quite early, the council-of-revision idea appeared several times. It was defeated each time. Ibid., pp. 166, 348-49, 428.

[9] Edward S. Corwin, *The President, Office and Powers 1787-1948*, 3d. ed. rev. (New York, N. Y.: New York University Press, 1948), p. 338.

[10] *The Federalist*, Number 51, p. 349.

sion of the veto constructed by the convention's Committee on Detail afforded insufficient protection. Thus,

> observing that if the negative of the President was confined to *bills*, it would be evaded by acts under the form and name of resolutions, votes, &c., [he] proposed that "or resolve" should be added after *"bill,"* in the beginning of Section 13, with an exception as to votes of adjournment.[11]

After a "short and rather confused conversation on the subject," Madison's proposal was defeated (three states in favor and eight opposed). The next day, Edmund Randolph, "having thrown into a new form" Madison's motion, offered it again. This time, it was accepted (nine states in favor and one opposed).[12]

The present language of the veto provision of Article I, Section 7, is as detailed and explicit as any provision of the Constitution. In addition, by Article II, Section 3, the President is admonished as part of his executive responsibilities to "take Care that the Laws be faithfully executed. . . ." This last duty is one of the *least* detailed and explicit of any provision of the Constitution. During the debates at the Constitutional Convention, considerable attention was given to the manner of selecting the President and the form that office should take; little attention was given to the exact scope of the President's official duties. But one of the Framers' concerns was that the President be capable of effective action. (Inferentially, their arguments support the notion that the executive must be allowed to function effectively once the legislature has acted.) In specifying what those functions are, Hamilton observed:

> The administration of government, in its largest sense, comprehends all the operations of the body politic, whether legislative, executive or judiciary, but in its most usual and perhaps in its most precise signification, it is limited to executive details, and falls peculiarly within the province of the executive department. The actual conduct of foreign negotiations, the preparatory plans of finance, the application and disbursement of the public monies in conformity to the general appropriations of the legislature, the arrangement of the army and navy, the direction of the operations of war; these and other matters of a like nature constitute what seems to be most properly understood by the administration of government.[13]

---

11 *Elliott's Debates*, vol. 5, p. 431 (emphasis in original).

12 Ibid.

13 *The Federalist*, Number 72, pp. 486-87.

It is against this background of the constitutional allocation of powers that the legislative veto should be examined.

Can the President Waive Executive Objections?

A threshold question is whether the President can waive his objections to the congressional veto by signing the legislation that embodies it. (A slightly more difficult, but not conceptually insuperable, problem is encountered by those who hold that a waiver is even possible if the President vetoes the offending legislation, but which is then passed over his veto. Since the constitutionally prescribed lawmaking path has been followed, and since the President's veto is not absolute but only qualified, the waiver theory is still valid.) Proponents of the legislative veto argue:

> The fact that a different President may have approved the act, or that the act may have been passed over a presidential veto does not take the force from this reasoning since the veto power belongs to the office, not the man, and since the possibility of a presidential veto being overridden is clearly contemplated by the Constitution.[14]

Justice Byron R. White in his separate opinion in *Buckley* v. *Valeo* made the same argument.[15]

That the waiver theory is untenable, however, was demonstrated by Justice White himself in an analogous case. In *United States* v. *Brewster*,[16] the Supreme Court faced the question whether the speech or debate clause (Article I, Section 6) barred the prosecution of a former senator on charges of bribes allegedly taken in exchange for his votes on certain issues. The Court held that the clause was no bar, and Justice White dissented. He argued that "a statute specifically including congressional conduct and purporting to be an exercise of congressional power to discipline its Members" violated the speech or debate clause, and added:

> I fail to understand how a majority of Congress can bind an objecting Congressman to a course so clearly at odds with the constitutional command that legislative conduct shall be subject to question in no place other than the Senate or the House of Representatives.[17]

---

[14] Joseph Cooper and Ann Cooper, "The Legislative Veto and the Constitution," *George Washington Law Review*, vol. 30 (1962), p. 478.

[15] 424 U.S. 1, 285 (White, J., concurring and dissenting).

[16] 408 U.S. 501 (1972).

[17] Ibid., p. 563 (White, J., dissenting).

Specifically,

> [t]he Speech or Debate Clause is an allocation of power. . . .
> A statute that represents an abdication of that power is in
> my view impermissible.[18]

Thus, when a constitutional provision allocates governmental power, it is not for even a majority of Congress to waive a privilege for another member or for future Congresses.

Similarly, the veto, also an allocation of governmental power, cannot be waived by a sitting President for himself, let alone for subsequent Presidents. Besides, as noted previously, the "acquiesence" of a President in a legislative veto is typically strained and reluctant at best. Subsequent to *Buckley* v. *Valeo*, the Supreme Court decided *National League of Cities* v. *Usery*,[19] in which it held that federal minimum wage laws could not constitutionally be applied to state and local government employees. In response to an argument in the dissenting opinion that because each state was entitled to two senators, the states were able to protect their own interests in the Congress and did not require the assistance of the judiciary, the Court relied on *Buckley* v. *Valeo*, and *Myers* v. *United States*.[20] It asserted that:

> In each of these cases, an even stronger argument than that
> made in the dissent could be made to the effect that since
> each of these bills had been signed by the President, the very
> officer who challenged them had consented to their becom-
> ing law, and it was therefore no concern of this Court that
> the law violated the Constitution. Just as the dissent con-
> tends that "the States are fully able to protect their own
> interests . . . ," it could have been contended that the
> President, armed with the mandate of a national constitu-
> ency and with the veto power, was able to protect *his* own
> interests. Nonetheless, in both cases the laws were held
> unconstitutional, because they trenched on the authority of
> the Executive Branch.[21]

Thus, no matter what the President does, his actions cannot protect the legislative veto if it is otherwise invalid.

---

18 Ibid. Justice William J. Brennan, Jr., joined by Justice William O. Douglas, also dissented, agreeing that speech or debate clause immunity could not be waived. Ibid., pp. 540-49 (Brennan, J., dissenting).

19 426 U.S. 833 (1976).

20 272 U.S. 52 (1926) (the President's authority to remove an *executive* officer appointed by him may not be limited by law).

21 426 U.S. 833, 841, n. 12 (emphasis in original).

The Separation of Powers

The main issue, however, is whether and to what extent the legislative veto disrupts the scheme of separation of powers. In practice, the congressional veto has two principal effects: first, it excludes the President from his proper role in the legislative process by foreclosing his use of the executive veto; and second, it impermissibly allows the legislature to intrude on functions assigned by the Constitution to the executive, namely, the carrying out and implementing of previously enacted legislation. Consideration of these twin abuses is often blurred in the literature,[22] but it is necessary to keep them analytically distinct. They represent two different constitutional violations. The first is an explicit violation of the veto power of Article I, Section 7. The second is a more general violation of the concept of the separation of powers, and particularly the requirement of Article II, Section 3, that the President ensure faithful execution of the laws.

The legislative veto eliminates the President from the lawmaking function by not presenting him with "legislation" that he can veto. It allows Congress to change its mind an unlimited number of times about what a statute is intended to do after passage of that statute—in effect, amending the statute.[23] So long as there is some reasonable connection between the statutory language and the regulations Congress eventually permits to be adopted, Congress has virtually unlimited power of amendment. Thus, the rules can be changed as time passes without having to overcome possible opposition from the executive branch, and "[i]t can hardly be gainsaid that resolutions secure passage more casually and less responsibly, in the main, than do enactments requiring presidential approval."[24] (With a one-house veto, of course, the task is even easier.) Moreover, by preventing regulations from taking effect, Congress may be able to exercise a partial repeal of certain statutes that are so general or so vague that they would be impossible practically to administrate or would risk constitutional invalidity because of excessive vagueness.

The President's administrative authority—his duty to "take Care that the Laws be faithfully executed"—is impinged because he is

---

[22] See, for example, Frank C. Newman and Harry J. Keaton, "Congress and the Faithful Execution of Laws—Should Legislators Supervise Administrators?" *California Law Review*, vol. 41 (1953), pp. 587-88.

[23] Representative Flowers asserted as much: ". . . it would seem that the veto power over administrative rules would really just be another aspect of the amendatory power that Congress inherently possesses." *Congressional Review of Administrative Rulemaking*, p. 381.

[24] United States v. Rumely, 345 U.S. 41, 46 (1953).

prevented from implementing regulations he deems suitable and consistent with the enabling legislation. Of course, it is rare that the President is directly responsible for specific regulations. But those who formulate the regulations are his designees and their assistants, very often constitutional Officers of the United States whom he has appointed.[25] Instead of these officials reviewing and approving regulations—subject always to judicial review—Congress intervenes to review the regulations, and possibly to prevent their taking effect. No one disputes that Congress could so intervene if it did so "by Law," as Article I puts it; that is, by amending the underlying statute, by fixing budget appropriations, and the like, or by confirming or not confirming appointments. If the Congress deems that the laws are not being "faithfully executed," it can make the laws more specific and bind the President more closely to its will. In extreme cases, it can impeach. What it cannot do is attempt to "execute" the laws itself, as when it decides whether or not particular regulations take effect.

Although supporters of the legislative veto often chide its opponents for being "formalistic" and overly mechanical in their interpretations of what constitutes an executive and what a legislative function,[26] the supporters themselves often argue on precisely that basis. They say that regulations are legislative, and thus justify congressional involvement in the executive at a very detailed level.[27] Regardless of the result of this ultimately sterile debate, the plain fact is that regulations are a necessary condition to the effective implementation of most statutes. Without regulations, citizens would often act at their peril as to what was permitted and what was not. Congress has several courses of action: it may enact the statutory standards in as much or as little detail as it chooses; it may delegate as much or as little authority to the executive as it desires; and it may amend later as much or as little as it wants. Once responsibility passes to the executive, however, Congress *cannot* take that responsibility back unless it is willing to submit to the possibility of a presidential veto.

---

25 As the Supreme Court said in Myers v. United States 272 U.S. 52, 163 (1926), and quoted approvingly in *Buckley*, "The president alone and unaided could not execute the laws. He must execute them by a system of subordinates." Buckley v. Valeo, 424 U.S. 1, 135.

26 Cooper and Cooper, "The Legislative Veto," note 57, pp. 480-87.

27 See, for example, statement of Representative Levitas, *Congressional Review of Administrative Rulemaking*, p. 155; Stewart, "Constitutionality of the Legislative Veto," note 43, p. 605.

This line of reasoning does not imply that congressional actions pertinent only to Congress—its internal or "housekeeping" resolutions—need be subject to a presidential veto. Those "which are peculiarly within the province of Congress alone" by long-standing custom and practice need not be submitted to the President.[28] The Supreme Court faced an analogous argument over the appointments clause in *Buckley*. The appellees contended that it "should not be read to exclude the 'inherent powers of Congress' to appoint its own officers to perform functions necessary to that body as an institution."[29] Holding that the six members of the Federal Election Commission (FEC) had to be appointed by the President, the Court nonetheless cautioned: "Contrary to the fears expressed by the majority of the Court of Appeals, nothing in our holding . . . will deny to Congress 'all power to appoint its own inferior officers to carry out appropriate legislative functions.'"[30] Likewise, a holding that one- or two-house legislative vetoes are unconstitutional would not require that congressional resolutions concerning necessary institutional functions be submitted to the President.

Despite the increasing frequency of its use recently, the legislative veto has never been adjudicated on constitutional grounds in the Supreme Court. The issue was explicitly raised by the plaintiffs in *Buckley* v. *Valeo*, along with their arguments that the mode of appointment of the six members of the FEC violated the separation of powers. The plaintiffs saw these two arguments as closely related, and indeed they are, both historically and conceptually. Because the Supreme Court found that the method of appointment was unconstitutional, however, it declined to reach the legislative-veto issue.[31] Nonetheless, the framework established by those portions of the opinion dealing with the appointment power provide considerable insight regarding possible Supreme Court treatment of an appropriate case in which the veto issue was raised.[32]

The opinion of the court in *Buckley* quoted approvingly from Chief Justice William H. Taft's opinion in *Hampton & Co.* v. *United States* to the effect that "in the actual administration of the government Congress or the Legislature should exercise the legislative power, the President or the State executive, the Governor, the execu-

---

[28] Statement of Assistant Attorney General Antonin Scalia, *Improving Congressional Oversight*, p. 126.

[29] 424 U.S. 1, 127.

[30] Ibid., p. 128.

[31] Ibid., p. 140, note 176.

[32] See "Congressional Veto of Administrative Action: The Probable Response to a Constitutional Challenge," *Duke Law Journal* (1976), p. 285.

tive power, and the Courts or the judiciary the judicial power"—a strict view of the separation of powers.[33] Chief Justice Taft's opinion warned that it was as impermissible for the Congress "to invest itself or its members with either executive power or judicial power" as it was for Congress to give up its legislative powers. Moreover, although the three branches were certainly coordinate, each could "invoke the action of the other two branches only in so far as the action invoked shall not be an assumption of the constitutional field of action of another branch."[34]

Again and again, the *Buckley* opinion emphasizes the importance of the separation of powers: it notes that the principle "was not an abstract generalization in the minds of the Framers," and warns that "[t]his Court has not hesitated to enforce" that principle.[35] The Court describes the appellees as contending "somewhat obliquely" that the appointments clause should be read so as not to exclude Congress, lest Congress be reduced in stature beside the other two branches. The opinion then sweeps those contentions aside, noting that "the debates of the Constitutional Convention, and the Federalist Papers, are replete with expressions of fear that the Legislative Branch of the National Government will aggrandize itself at the expense of the other two branches."[36] This is not the stuff from which much judicial sympathy for the legislative veto emerges.

When the necessary and proper clause of Article I was invoked as justifying the mode of appointment to the FEC, the Court answered summarily.[37] Similar arguments made by proponents of the legislative veto [38] will likely meet the same fate.

Most pertinent to a consideration of the legislative veto is the Supreme Court's treatment of the FEC's powers to make rules and whether such powers could be exercised by an appointed commission. Noting that the powers to make rules and formulate advisory opinions were more legislative and judicial in nature than the commission's powers of civil enforcement, the Court then stated:

---

[33] 424 U.S. 1, 121, quoting Hampton & Co. v. United States, 276 U.S. 394, 406 (1928). In Springer v. Philippine Islands, 277 U.S. 189, 202 (1928), also quoted approvingly in *Buckley*, the Court again said "[l]egislative power, as distinguished from executive power, is the authority to make laws, but not to enforce them or appoint agents charged with the duty of such enforcement. The latter are executive functions."

[34] 424 U.S. 1, 122, quoting Hampton & Co. v. United States.

[35] Ibid., pp. 123-24.

[36] Ibid., pp. 128-29.

[37] Ibid., pp. 134-35.

[38] See, for example, Memorandum for Senator Charles H. Percy (Republican, Illinois), reprinted in *Improving Congressional Oversight*, p. 93.

each of these functions also represents the performance of a significant governmental duty exercised pursuant to a public law. . . . [N]one of them operates merely in aid of congressional authority to legislate or is sufficiently removed from the administration and enforcement of public law to allow it to be performed by the present Commission.[39]

Although the *Buckley* holding is limited to the appointment power, the implication from the language just quoted is that the rule-making function is so intimately tied to the executive's responsibilities that Congress may intervene only in a fashion explicitly sanctioned by the Constitution. Making of rules and granting of advisory opinions are thus closely tied to the "administration and enforcement of public law," that is, to the basic presidential responsibility to "take Care that the Laws be faithfully executed."

Even though the FEC is an "independent" agency and thus not directly subject to the President's control, its "administration and enforcement" of a statute are virtually identical to the roles of the more purely "executive" agencies. Strictly speaking, an independent agency's "executive" duties are not encompassed in the President's responsibility to ensure faithful execution of the laws, but they are functionally the same. Congressional interference with the "executive" responsibilities of the independent agencies is thus just as deleterious as similar interference with the responsibilities of the executive departments themselves. Political accountability to the President aside, therefore, the rationale for not permitting the legislature to interfere with the administration of statutes is equally applicable whether an agency is executive or independent. In any event, an attempt by Congress effectively to alter the statute and circumvent the presidential veto, no matter what the characterization of the enforcement agency, is still unconstitutional.[40]

Unlike the other members of the Court, Justice White, in his separate opinion in *Buckley* v. *Valeo*, did reach the constitutionality of the congressional veto. He would have sustained it. Likewise, in *Clark* v. *Valeo*, only Judge George E. MacKinnon addressed the con-

---

[39] 424 U.S. 1, 141.

[40] It may well be that the *Buckley* decision represents a withdrawal from some of the more expansive language in Humphrey's Executor v. United States, 295 U.S. 602 (1935), which characterized the Federal Trade Commission as "an agency of the legislative or judicial departments of the government." Moreover, the distinction between "independent" and "executive" agencies is often completely obscured in practice. See Gellhorn and Byse, *Administrative Law*, pp. 97–109.

stitutional merits and he would have held the legislative veto invalid.[41] That case was brought by former Attorney General Ramsey Clark against the legislative-veto provisions of the Federal Election Campaign Act. A majority of the District of Columbia Circuit held that the issue of the legislative veto was not ripe for decision. Judge MacKinnon's dissent in *Clark* v. *Valeo* is particularly noteworthy since he also dissented when his court found that the appointments clause issue was not ripe in *Buckley*. That holding was reversed by the Supreme Court, which substantially adopted Judge MacKinnon's dissenting views on appeal.[42]

Justice White rests his argument primarily on the fact that the Federal Election Campaign Act's legislative veto is passive. The proposed regulations take effect unless one house or the other passes a resolution disapproving them. Thus,

> [t]he regulation becomes effective by nonaction. . . . Congressional influence over the substantive content of agency regulation may be enhanced, but I would not view the power of either House to disapprove as equivalent to legislation or to an order, resolution or vote requiring the concurrence of both Houses.[43]

He elaborated this position by noting that

> [i]t would be considerably different if Congress itself purported to adopt and propound regulations by the actions of both Houses. But here no action of either House is required for the agency rule to go into effect, and the veto power of the President does not appear to be implicated.[44]

As noted previously, Justice White also subscribed to the theory that the President's approval of legislation establishing the veto (or the passing of such legislation over the veto) validates such a provision.

In Justice White's view, therefore, two factors distinguish a one-house legislative veto from those actions constitutionally required to be submitted to the President: first, if neither house acts, the regulations take effect as if there were no legislative-veto provision; and second, only one house need disapprove to nullify the proposed

---

41 Clark v. Valeo, Civil No. 76-1227 (D. C. Cir., January 21, 1977) (MacKinnon, J., dissenting).

42 424 U.S. 1, 109-43.

43 Ibid., pp. 284-85 (White, J., concurring and dissenting).

44 Ibid., p. 286. Justice White did agree that the main purpose of the presidential veto was to "shore up the Executive Branch and to provide it with some bargaining and survival power against what the Framers feared would be the overweening power of legislators."

regulation, unlike legislation, which requires the concurrence of both houses. Before the erroneousness of these distinctions is examined, what Justice White did *not* say should be emphasized. He did not say that *all* forms of the legislative veto were constitutional. Indeed, his framework all but demands finding unconstitutional a requirement that *both* houses approve a regulation before it becomes effective. Such a provision looks as if Congress purports "to adopt and propound regulations by the action of both Houses." Similarly, even a requirement that *one* house expressly approve a regulation before it takes effect also appears unconstitutional because the regulation does *not* "become effective by nonaction." Thus, even under Justice White's approach legislative vetoes that require that regulations be explicitly *approved* by one house are invalid.

Having thus delimited the scope of Justice White's views, we consider his two reasons why the President's veto can be permissibly avoided. First, because it is inaction that results in regulations taking effect, there is nothing for the President's veto to act on. But this tells only half the story. If the regulations *are* vetoed, then surely the Congress has acted just as emphatically as if it explicitly approved regulations, which even Justice White is not prepared to defend as constitutional. Moreover, the distinction between active and passive is without constitutional import for another reason: inaction rather than action is merely for the convenience of Congress. Rather than having to submit to the tedious mechanics of routinely approving massive amounts of noncontroversial regulations, Congress need only energize itself with respect to specifically troublesome proposed rules.

The "convenience" of making proposed regulations subject to the legislative veto while permitting them to take effect unless explicitly disapproved is exemplified by the statutes governing congressional pay increases.[45] Under those provisions, the President, after receiving the reports of the Commission on Executive, Legislative and Judicial Salaries, may transmit to Congress recommendations for broad-ranging salary alterations. Those recommendations become effective unless one house of Congress disapproves of them.[46] Representative John J. Rhodes (Republican, Arizona), minority leader

---

[45] 2 U.S.C., sections 31, 351–61.

[46] The statute actually provides two alternatives. 2 U.S.C., section 359. Congress may either enact a new statute establishing rates of pay (a constitutional way to proceed) or one house may specifically disapprove "all or part of" the recommendation. Although the subsection referring to the one-house veto calls such action "legislation," the label is plainly inaccurate since only one house need act. In practice, one-house disapproval has not been treated as "legislation."

of the House of Representatives, described the statutory provision and related procedural rules as having

> virtually ensured approval of all pay raises. It also spared Members the embarrassment of having to vote themselves a pay increase. They could tell the people in their district that they were dead set against the raise but were powerless to change "the system." [47]

Why buttressing congressional inertia becomes a constitutional justification for a passive legislative-veto system is nowhere explained in Justice White's opinion. And, as noted previously, the intimidating effect of the *potential* for a veto may accomplish all that is necessary in any event.

If Justice White's rationalization and the foregoing discussion appear somewhat jesuitical, then it is surely a good demonstration of Madison's warning: because the constitutional powers of the legislature are "more extensive" and "less susceptible of precise limits," the Congress "can with the greater facility, *mask under complicated and indirect measures, the encroachments which it makes on the co-ordinate departments.*" [48] As Judge MacKinnon has recently put it, "[t]he vices of the one-house veto scheme are as subtle as they are numerous." [49]

Justice White's second reason why the President's veto can be avoided is based upon the fact that only one house need act for regulations to be vetoed. To be sure, Article I, Section 7, does speak of measures that need the concurrence of both—rather than merely one—of the houses. But as one commentator observed before the *Buckley* decision,

> [i]t verges on irrationality to maintain that action by con- current resolution, whereby Congress is at least held in check by its own structure, is invalid because the veto clause so states, but that the invalidity of a simple resolution,

---

47 John J. Rhodes, *The Futile System* (McLean, Va.: EPM Publications, Inc., 1976), p. 60.

48 *The Federalist*, Number 48, p. 334 (emphasis added).

49 Clark v. Valeo (MacKinnon, Jr., dissenting, slip opinion, p. 19, n. 16). Judge MacKinnon's treatment of Justice White's attempted distinction between con- gressional action and nonaction is as persuasive as it is blunt: "to assert that Congress does nothing when the vote or action of Congress is to *not veto* a regulation is merely to play with words and to deny reality. Such interpretation of the legislative situation incorrectly describes what happens when Congress decides to *not veto* a regulation. That result is definite action—'not nonaction.'" In this pragmatic and realistic view of how Congress actually functions, much of Justice White's analysis becomes purely academic.

wherein a single House acts without check, is more in doubt.[50]

It surely must be true that a power not permitted to both houses of Congress by the Constitution cannot suddenly be made available by delegating it to one house. Article I, Section 1, is uncomplicated and straightforward: "All legislative Powers herein granted shall be vested in a Congress of the United States, which shall consist of a Senate and a House of Representatives." The principle of bicameralism was of immense importance to the Framers, both for reasons of federalism—so that the small states would be able to have a significant voice despite their lesser populations—and because of the desire to keep the legislative power in check. To disregard these concerns would be to cast aside one of the most fundamental decisions of the Constitutional Convention. Indeed, for these reasons, if the two-house legislative veto is unconstitutional, the one-house veto would seem even more clearly unconstitutional.

The Supreme Court has already, in effect, so indicated. The opinion in *Kilbourn* v. *Thompson*, states that "[o]f course, neither branch of Congress, when acting separately, can lawfully exercise more power than is conferred by the Constitution on the whole body, except in the few instances where authority is conferred on either House separately, as in the case of impeachments." [51] No one claims that the legislative veto is explicitly authorized by the Constitution, let alone that a one-house veto is permissible because of a power separately given to either house acting alone.

The Contingency and Delegation of Power Arguments

A final argument that is occasionally raised in defense of the legislative veto is that it is merely an arrangement similar to those statutes providing that agencies should (or should not) take certain actions upon the occurrence of specific events.[52] The concept of permitting the executive to exercise delegated legislative authority only upon the happening of certain contingencies was one theory used early on to

---

[50] Watson, "Congress Steps Out," p. 1066, n. 428.

[51] 103 U.S. 168, 182. The Court in *Kilbourn* echoed the sentiments of Madison, who felt that the legislature was apt to dominate the other branches, and that "[t]he remedy for this inconveniency is, to divide the legislature into different branches." *The Federalist*, Number 51, p. 350.

[52] See, for example, statements of Senator Sam J. Ervin (Democrat, North Carolina) in *Hearings before the Subcommittee on Separation of Powers of the Senate Judiciary Committee*, 90th Congress, 1st session, part I, pp. 122-28 (1967).

validate delegations of power. Its applicability to the legislative veto is, however, not apparent. As one commentator pointed out:

> It is one thing for Congress to enact legislation which is contingent upon the occurrence of certain events or upon the determination of certain facts by executive officers or even the vote of certain groups of the population; it is quite another thing for Congress to reserve to itself the right to determine whether an executive decision made in pursuance of the law shall be carried out.[53]

In the first instance, "the condition is external to Congress and its action is complete when the legislation is enacted"; in the second instance, "the condition involves the future decision by Congress itself."[54] In effect, Congress is arguing that it be allowed to change the rules as the game progresses. That would be an unexceptionable argument *if* Congress were following the constitutionally prescribed path of legislation. By excluding the executive from participating, however, Congress has made the "contingency" depend only on a change in its own mind.

A related argument is that, if Congress is permitted to delegate authority, it is likewise permitted to attach conditions to that delegation.[55] At best, this is begging the question. If Congress were to delegate certain power to an agency on the condition that no Jew ever hold an office in that agency, the condition would obviously be unconstitutional. The fact that it was attached to an otherwise legitimate delegation could not in any way save it. So, too, with the legislative veto. Indeed, the opposite might be true; if it were held that the veto and the delegation could not be severed, the delegation might fall as well. Some observers have suggested that, if the President were to be given substantial control over the actions of independent agencies, and if the President's action were to be subject to the congressional veto, then the statute itself should make clear that the delegation of power and the legislative veto were *not* severable. Thus, if the legislative veto were struck down, the delegation would also fall. Congress would then not be left in a position of having delegated power but without the veto.[56] As this proposal indicates by its very terms, the "condition" argument is a makeweight at best.

---

[53] Harris, *Congressional Control of Administration*, p. 241.
[54] Ibid.
[55] Statement of Representative Levitas in *Congressional Review of Administrative Rulemaking*, p. 156.
[56] Testimony of Lloyd N. Cutler, in *Improving Congressional Oversight*, pp. 15-16.

Unfortunately, however, it may have a significant impact on Congress. If the veto is viewed as a check on the power delegated, Congress may be tempted to cede more power to the executive than it might otherwise. One commentator has warned that following such logic

> the two branches considered as a unit exercise a power greater than that which would be possible without passive control. This expansion of federal power is precisely what the Framers sought to avoid in placing the power to legislate and the power to execute the laws in different hands.[57]

The expansion of federal power is, of course, a concern different from a distortion of the proper allocation of power (however much there is) among the branches. Use of the legislative veto, ironically, may result in consequences that are the exact reverse of those sought by its proponents: even if Congress gains power relative to the executive, it may grant the government more control over its citizens' lives rather than less.

Certain devices frequently resorted to by the Congress have been equated with the legislative veto, thus causing much unnecessary confusion. One is the so-called report-and-wait provision. Under this requirement, an agency must submit proposed regulations to Congress and then wait a specified period before the regulations go into effect.[58] If Congress disapproves of the regulations, it may enact new legislation modifying the statutes under which the regulations were promulgated. Like all other legislation, such actions would have to be approved by both houses and by the President (or passed over his veto).

The report-and-wait mechanism is probably constitutional, and the opinion of the District of Columbia Circuit in *Clark* v. *Valeo* so stated.[59] Unlike the legislative veto, it does not exclude the President from the legislative process. Moreover, by creating a mechanism whereby regulations are necessarily brought to the attention of Congress, it increases the chance that regulations contrary to the legislative intent will be noticed. If that is truly what proponents of the legislative veto desire, they will be afforded an open opportunity to

---

[57] Watson, "Congress Steps Out," p. 1081. While Watson limits his comment to one-house expressions of disapproval of proposed executive action, its logic applies to all manifestations of the legislative veto.

[58] See Ginnane, "Control of Federal Administration," note 18, pp. 577-78, 601-03.

[59] Clark v. Valeo, slip opinion, p. 13. Judge MacKinnon argued forcefully that "there is a radical difference in kind between the influence of a *one-house veto* and any simple lay-over provision." (MacKinnon, J., dissenting, slip opinion, p. 6, note 4.)

enact amendatory legislation. The report-and-wait procedure is more cumbersome than the legislative veto, but the separation of powers was not designed for its efficiency.[60]

Report-and-wait provisions have received some attention in the past. The Federal Rules of Civil Procedure were promulgated under such a system.[61] Rules prescribed by the Supreme Court take effect only after having been reported to Congress by the Chief Justice and after ninety days have passed. Most such proposed rules have simply been permitted to become effective. Because, however, several of the proposed Federal Rules of Evidence aroused considerable controversy, Congress by law prevented those rules from taking effect "except to the extent, and with such amendments, as they may be expressly approved by an Act of Congress." [62] After deliberation and some amendments, Congress enacted its version of the Rules of Evidence, and that legislation was signed by the President.[63]

Even if it is constitutional, the report-and-wait procedure has many of the practical defects of the legislative veto. It will likely be used only sporadically, and it may well permit nearly as much interference with agency procedures as the veto. Presumably, however, such interference could occur even without a report-and-wait provision. If a member of Congress had an offensive regulation brought to his attention, he might well be in a position to hold hearings on the subject, or he might apply any number of pressure or persuasion techniques to the executive or independent agency to have the regulations changed.[64] The report-and-wait provision thus only formalizes a mode of legislative oversight that already exists. The executive branch in effect has already recognized this point. President Herbert

[60] "The doctrine of the separation of powers was adopted by the Convention of 1787, not to promote efficiency but to preclude the exercise of arbitrary power. The purpose was, not to avoid friction, but, by means of the inevitable friction incident to the distribution of the governmental powers among three departments, to save the people from autocracy." Myers v. United States, 272 U.S. 52, 293 (1926) (Brandeis, J., dissenting).

[61] P.L. No. 73-415, 48 Stat. 1064 (1934), now amended and codified at 28 U.S.C., section 2072. In Sibbach v. Wilson & Co., 312 U.S. 1, 15 (1940), in considering the validity of one of the new Rules, the Court spoke favorably of the report-and-wait procedure. Unfortunately, however, it cited as analogous precedent legislative-veto provisions in the reorganization acts. The constitutionality of neither procedure was before the Court in Sibbach v. Wilson, and there was little, if any, academic commentary on the legislative veto at that time.

[62] P.L. No. 93-12, 87 Stat. 9 (1973).

[63] P.L. No. 93-595, 88 Stat. 1926 (1975); *Weekly Compilation of Presidential Documents*, vol. 11 (1975), p. 12.

[64] Justice White, writing for the Court in Gravel v. United States, 408 U.S. 606, 625 (1972) specifically noted that legislators are "constantly in touch" with the executive branch.

C. Hoover's attorney general observed that "[n]o one would question the power of Congress to provide for delay in the execution of such an administrative order, or its power to withdraw the authority to make the order, provided the withdrawal takes the form of legislation."[65] President Franklin Roosevelt supported a version of what later became the Reorganization Act of 1939, and that contained a report-and-wait section.[66]

The Reorganization Acts

The reorganization acts themselves pose interesting questions and deserve separate consideration because of recent controversy over their merits. There was at one time general statutory authority (since expired) for reorganization of the executive branch.[67] Specific authorizations have been made for general reorganization.[68] There has also been legislation for particular departments and agencies.[69] Commentators are divided on the constitutionality of the reorganization acts because of their special involvement with the internal structure of the executive branch.[70] President Jimmy Carter's announced intention is to pattern his proposed reorganization act after past acts that contain a legislative veto.[71]

---

[65] 37 Ops. Atty. Gen. 56, 63 (1933).

[66] The presidential message containing these sentiments is reprinted in *Congressional Record*, vol. 83 (1938), p. 4487.

[67] 5 U.S.C., sections 901-13, which largely codifies the Reorganization Act of 1949. The codification was accomplished by P.L. No. 89-554, 8th Stat. 378, 393-98 (1966).

[68] Legislative Appropriations Act of 1932, 47 Stat. 414 (1932); Reorganization Act of 1939, 53 Stat. 561-62 (1939); Reorganization Act of 1945, P.L. No. 263, 59 Stat. 616 (1945); Reorganization Act of 1949, P.L. No. 109, 63 Stat. 205 (1949).

[69] See, for example, Department of Defense Reorganization Act of 1958, P.L. No. 85-599, 72 Stat. 514-15 (1958); Arms Control and Disarmament Act, P.L. No. 87-297, 75 Stat. 636 (1961); Equal Employment Opportunity Act of 1972, P.L. No. 92-261, 86 Stat. 103 (1972).

[70] The late Professor Alexander Bickel believed that the legislative-veto provisions of the reorganization acts were unconstitutional, *Hearings before the Subcommittee on Separation of Powers*, pp. 250-52; as does former Assistant Attorney General Scalia, *Improving Congressional Oversight*, pp. 87-88, and Ginnane, "Control of Federal Administration," pp. 593-95. Watson, "Congress Steps Out," pp. 1076-78, has a different view. See also, *The Executive Reorganization Act: A Survey of Proposals for Renewal and Modification* (Washington, D.C.: American Enterprise Institute, 1977).

[71] David Broder, "Carter to Support Year's Extension of Key Programs," *Washington Post*, January 11, 1976, p. A1.

Generally, the reorganization acts have delegated broad authority to the President to plan and later implement changes in the executive branch. He may typically transfer functions from one agency to another, consolidate existing agencies, abolish old departments, and create new ones. Previous reorganization acts have been motivated by considerations of reducing federal expenditures, increasing the efficiency of the government, promoting better execution of the laws, and reducing overlapping and duplicative efforts. There is no convincing reason, however, why reorganizations of the executive branch should not be treated in the same way as more substantive legislation. A colloquy between former Senator Sam J. Ervin (Democrat, North Carolina) and the late Professor Alexander M. Bickel emphasizes the similarity in principle of the reorganization acts and more substantive statutes:

> PROFESSOR BICKEL. . . . I know that [the approach of the reorganization act] has been in effect and it has entered the practice of the Constitution if not its theory for over a generation now. However, I cannot reconcile it with my view of the requirements of the separation of powers. . . .

> SENATOR ERVIN. I have convinced myself to this point. If the principle of the Reorganization Acts is constitutional, then a comparable procedure allowing Congress to veto watershed projects conceived by the Executive is also constitutional.

> PROFESSOR BICKEL. I quite agree.

> SENATOR ERVIN. And if the latter is unconstitutional then the former is unconstitutional.

> PROFESSOR BICKEL. I quite agree with that.[72]

The structure of the government is certainly the proper concern of both the Congress and the President. No loss of presidential authority is entailed by congressional passage of detailed reorganization statutes, any more than when Congress creates a new agency by statute. Moreover, the underlying rationales for reorganization of the executive branch described above indicate how intimately connected restructuring proposals are with "substantive" legislation.

In fact, Congress has in the past explicitly directed the President to make certain structural changes in the executive. In the Legislative Appropriations Act of 1932, for instance, Congress directed the secretary of commerce to consolidate the Steamboat Inspection Service

---

[72] *Hearings before the Subcommittee on Separation of Powers*, pp. 250-51.

and the Bureau of Navigation into one agency, it abolished the Personnel Classification Board and transferred its functions to the Civil Service Commission, and it abolished the Radio Division of the Department of Commerce and transferred its functions to the Federal Radio Commission (which itself later became the Federal Communications Commission).[73] In addition, these and numerous other statutes plainly refute the idea that there is any "inherent" presidential power to rearrange the bureaucracy without the effective participation of Congress. Congress is perfectly able and sufficiently expert to be involved in reorganizations if it so chooses. It is hard to believe that Congress would not listen most carefully to any proposals offered by the President, or that it would act capriciously contrary to his wishes. But there is certainly no reason to leave the entire job exclusively to him, subject only to later congressional veto. Indeed, the whole process sounds somewhat backwards, and objection has been raised to the reorganization plans exactly because so much legislative authority is conceded to the President.

There is a substantial additional risk posed by the traditional formulation of the reorganization acts. Should the legislative veto be declared unconstitutional, or should it be held that the delegation of power to the President were invalid, the entire reorganization plan would be in jeopardy. Since any decision would come only after significant rearrangement had likely already occurred, such a decision would have grave consequences, and it would perhaps cause serious impairment to the workings of many governmental agencies. Why such an immense risk should be incurred when the constitutionally safe alternative of following the normal legislative process (with considerable presidential advice) is easily available has nowhere been explained.

In any event, the one-house veto (the mechanism proposed by President Carter) is actually quite a paltry weapon during a time of massive reorganization. Representative Jack Brooks (Democrat, Texas), for instance, recently noted that eliminating the legislative-veto mechanism and requiring actual legislation would "make Congress a full partner in carrying out its constitutional role."[74] Defense of including the legislative veto in the reorganization act rests only on the notion that the plans would not "result in increased exercise of federal power."[75] Such reasoning ignores the crucial point that the

---

[73] 47 Stat. 415-17 (1932).

[74] Broder, "Brooks Balks at Carter Bill on Reorganization Powers," *Washington Post*, January 14, 1976, p. A2.

[75] Watson, "Congress Steps Out," p. 1077.

allocation of power among the branches is just as important as the total amount of that power. Congress would be well advised to consider reorganizations of the executive branch in the same fashion in which it considers other legislation. In fact, a debate over a reorganization act would be a true test of the seriousness of those who argue for a more accountable executive branch. There is no better time for Congress to regain its status as a "full partner" of the President than by insisting on an integral role in any restructuring plan.

Pending Litigation

Several cases that are now in litigation may provide answers to at least some of these constitutional issues within the relatively near future. *Clark* v. *Valeo*, discussed previously, concerns the Federal Election Campaign Act's legislative veto. This case raises not only the constitutionality of the legislative veto generally but also the issue of whether the First Amendment rights of candidates who are not incumbents are infringed by giving their opponents effective control over the Federal Election Commission's regulations.[76] The plaintiffs have recently appealed to the Supreme Court.[77] Even if the Court notes probable jurisdiction, however, it is likely to consider only those issues deemed to be ripe by the Court of Appeals. Should the plaintiffs succeed in the Supreme Court, new briefs would probably be ordered and the case would be reargued on the merits before the Court of Appeals.

Purely in terms of the time involved to accomplish these maneuvers, therefore, the first case to reach the Supreme Court on the merits might well be *Atkins* v. *United States*.[78] In that case eighty-two sitting federal judges are asserting that Article III, Section 1, has been violated by congressional failure to provide pay increases for judges to match the rate of inflation. Article II provides that judicial compensation "shall not be diminished" during a judge's term in office, and a proposed pay increase for judges was prevented by a one-house legislative veto. In light of the constitutional issues raised not only by the compensation question but also by the legisla-

---

[76] Judge MacKinnon noted in his Court of Appeals opinion that "from the beginning the Act was dripping with features that sought to exert congressional control over the normal functioning of the Commission." Clark v. Valeo (MacKinnon, J., dissenting, slip opinion, p. 7).

[77] 45 U.S. L.W. 3544 (February 15, 1977).

[78] Ct. Cl. No. 41-76, together with Bechtle v. United States, Ct. Cl. No. 132-76, and Aldisert v. United States, Ct. Cl. No. 357-76.

tive veto, the House of Representatives and Senate were invited to, and did, file amicus curiae (friend of the court) briefs.[79] In oral argument before the Supreme Court in *Buckley*, Justice Rehnquist hypothesized that, if the legislative veto were unconstitutional, "all of the Associate Justices of this Court would apparently still be making $39,000 a year, wouldn't they. I mean all the Federal Salary Acts provide for one-house veto." [80] *Atkins* has already been to the Supreme Court once on a collateral issue, has been argued before the Court of Claims, and is now under advisement there.[81]

---

[79] Briefs were filed on behalf of Nelson A. Rockefeller as President of the Senate, and Frank Thompson, Jr., as Chairman of the House Committee on Administration.

[80] Oral argument tr. 161.

[81] The judges of the Court of Claims certified to the Supreme Court the question whether they were allowed to decide the case (under the "doctrine of necessity"), since a result favorable to the plaintiffs would obviously augment their own compensation. The Supreme Court dismissed the certificate with three Justices (Lewis F. Powell, Potter Stewart, and John P. Stevens) dissenting. 426 U.S. 944 (1976). A holding by the Court of Claims that it was precluded from reaching the merits because of the possible conflict of interest might well delay resolution of the legislative-veto issues until after an appeal to the Supreme Court on the jurisdictional question.

CONCLUSION

The story of the legislative veto is a depressing story—depressing because, although the goals sought through the use of the device are commendable, the device itself is, almost necessarily, unconstitutional. Moreover, the goals—greater agency accountability and less arbitrary governmental interference in people's lives—might be harder to reach with the legislative veto than without it because it tends to give the false impression that the agencies are under control. In order for those worthy goals to be achieved, Congress must be willing (or be forced) to make difficult political choices. Statutory grants of discretion must be more carefully structured and periodically reviewed. More attention must be paid to specifics, closer scrutiny must be given to presidential nominees, and there needs to be greater resistance to calls for "immediate legislative action" from interested pressure groups.

It is not enough to hope that the legislative veto will only be employed against the most egregious agency proposals. Supporters of the veto candidly agree with its detractors in saying that "the veto conceivably could be used to deliver the executive completely or substantially into the hands of Congress." [1] With so much potential for abuse in itself, the legislative veto seems hardly appropriate as a remedy for the abuses perpetrated by the executive and independent agencies. Rather than carping about particular obnoxious regulations, and rather than decrying new diminutions in personal freedom, Congress should more seriously engage in its primary function—lawmaking. It can bring overweening agencies strictly into line by passing proper legislation, and it should do so—but in a way con-

---

[1] Cooper and Cooper, "The Legislative Veto," note 57, p. 505.

sistent with Article I's vesting of the Congress with *legislative* powers. So doing would make more difficult greater concessions of power to the federal government, while also ensuring that the proper balance of power among the three branches would be preserved.

The Legislative Veto: Unseparating the Powers by John R. Bolton examines the practical and constitutional difficulties inherent in the currently popular idea of giving one or both houses of Congress a "veto" over proposed executive branch actions. In the author's view, the legislative veto could result in a misallocation of power among the branches of the federal government and an overall increase in federal power. He argues that the veto violates the constitutional doctrine of separation of powers, whether substantive measures or reorganization acts are involved.

John R. Bolton, a Washington attorney, was one of the counsel for James Buckley and Eugene McCarthy in their suit against the Federal Election Campaign Act and its amendments. He is the author of *The Hatch Act: A Civil Libertarian Defense* (American Enterprise Institute, 1976).

$2.25

 American Enterprise Institute for Public Policy Research
1150 Seventeenth Street, N.W., Washington, D.C. 20036